Dorothea Katharina Schmidt

Weaving Paper

13 Upcycled Projects with Scrap Paper

SCHIFFER CRAFT

4880 Lower Valley Road • Atglen, PA 19310

Contents

Basic Basket—
Your First Project

Starring Role—
A Tray

A Flowery Box
on the Shelf

Desk Organizer

Welcome

I'm really happy that you're interested in handmade baskets and have found this book!

Even if you have never woven a basket, this book is right for you. I will explain the techniques of paper weaving to you, starting with the basics. You don't need any prior knowledge. When I began to weave paper baskets, I didn't have anybody to show me how. Therefore, it took several attempts before I was happy with the results. I know how to avoid beginners' mistakes. With my instructions, your first project will be a success.

Maybe you have already woven baskets using willow or wicker, and you know the techniques used for weaving, rims, and bottoms. This book is also right for you because it includes a whole host of tips and tricks, which are particularly interesting for paper weaving. Furthermore, you will probably also discover something new, thanks to the colorful design possibilities offered by paper.

When I was making the baskets for this book at home, I sometimes imagined that I was sitting at a large table with everyone who would use this book as a reference for weaving paper. In my mind's eye I saw a long table bathed in sunlight with lots of cups of tea or coffee, cookies, laughter, a babble of voices, a pile of newspapers, glue, and a whole array of paper objects. A fantastic image! I invite you to sit at this imaginary table with me and to start weaving paper baskets. It is unbelievably good fun!

Cordially,

Dorothea

The Basic Techniques

The simple principle of using paper to weave baskets:
to create the paper rolls, cut some paper into strips, roll the strips into thin rolls, and stick them together with glue. The rolls are both flexible and stable and can be endlessly inserted into each other, making them the perfect material for weaving.

1. The Materials

1.1 Newspaper

Normal newspapers are well suited for basket weaving because the large sheets of paper produce very long rolls. Additionally, rolls made from newspaper are particularly soft, have a comfortable feel, and are easy to work with. Newspaper has an even thickness and quality, which is beneficial when you want to make a large number of similar rolls to weave. Furthermore, the woven newspaper can be easily painted.

Finished woven works made of newspaper that are not painted generally appear gray white, and sometimes, colorful spots are also visible (fig. 1). If you don't like the appearance, you can also make white rolls from newspaper. You can influence the color of the paper rolls as you roll them (see p. 34).

1.2 Magazines

Magazines with staples in the center are well suited for basket weaving. Once you remove the staples, you normally have an A3 sheet that can be made into really long rolls. The paper quality of magazines can vary from thick, glossy paper to transparent, thin paper of very poor quality. Generally, very thick paper is harder to work with than thin paper. The rolls made of thick paper can be so stiff that they break when weaving.

If you want to weave with magazines, you should collect enough magazines of a similar or the same paper quality. If you combine soft, flexible rolls from cheap TV magazines with hard, shiny rolls from glossy magazines in your weave, you could end up with an irregular and unsatisfactory result.

All in all, the appearance of baskets made from magazines is more colorful than those made from newspapers (fig. 2).

1.3 Advertising leaflets

Advertising leaflets from the daily or weekly newspapers have two special characteristics. First, they're sometimes very big and therefore allow particularly long rolls to be produced. Second, these leaflets are often super colorful right to the edges, which gives the finished paper weave a colorful appearance. Otherwise, the same applies to them as applies to newspapers.

1.4 Material and tools

• a thin metal skewer (or a knitting needle or similar)
• glue stick
• scissors
• scrap paper
• a paper or wooden base for the basket in the desired size, if you don't want to weave the basket base

• paint or varnish (and the tools needed to apply the paint; see p. 34)

• a punch or a hole punch (in the case of a wooden base, a drill, to put holes in the edges of the base; alternatively, a stapler to staple the stakes and spokes to the paper base)

• a ruler to measure the strips of newspaper

• a thin, flat object (e.g., a knife, a letter opener, or small pair of scissors) to push the paper rolls into the weave (e.g., when finishing off the rim)

• liquid glue or superglue to secure things if required

• florist's wire in order to stabilize points that will be exposed to loads and stresses or to add shape

• pegs to temporarily secure things

• masking tape to secure things (e.g., when making a handle)

Tip

You'll learn on p. 34 how to influence the color of the basket while making the rolls from newspaper, magazines, or advertising leaflets.

2. Making the Rolls

2.1 Technique

To begin with, you'll need a large amount of paper strips. All strips should be of more or less the same quality and width. They don't have to be exactly the same, just roughly.

Open magazines at the center and remove the staples. For thin paper, it's enough to simply cut it in half (fig. 1). For thick, glossy paper, the rolls would become too stiff if you only cut the paper in half. Therefore, cut the sheets into three strips of approximately equal width.

Cut newspaper into strips lengthways. A width of about 5 or 6 inches creates perfect rolls. For many daily newspapers you'll get 5.5-inch-wide strips if you cut the sheets into equal widths (fig. 2). Of course, you don't need to open the paper before cutting it (fig. 3). Find the most effective way to make strips from your newspaper.

PRACTICAL TIP: When paper is produced, the individual paper fibers are pointing in a specific direction. That means that the paper often behaves differently when it is rolled, depending on whether the strips have been cut horizontally or vertically from the paper. It's good practice to roll a "test strip" to discover how to handle the paper best. Some paper simply scrunches or crinkles—don't waste time with that; just find something else.

How to make the paper rolls

Place a strip of paper crossways in front of you on the edge of the table. Starting from the lower left corner, roll the strip tightly over a skewer, while gently pressing the growing paper roll on the table. Make sure that the skewer is positioned almost parallel to the lower edge of the strip (fig. 4). While rolling, the angle will automatically become somewhat bigger. So that the thicker end of the skewer can also move, let it hang slightly over the edge of the table (figs. 5–6). Spread some glue over the last corner of the paper before you finish rolling (fig. 7). Pull out the skewer, and ta-da!

Don't feel disheartened if at first you don't roll with the speed and accuracy of a production line—once you have had a little practice, you will get the knack of it.

When you look closely at the finished rolls, you'll see that they have one pointed end and one funnel-shaped end (fig. 8). The pointed end of one roll can be carefully inserted and "screwed" into the funnel-shaped end of the next roll to create a secure connection between the two rolls.

If you are struggling to connect the paper rolls

- Insert the skewer into the funnel-shaped end of the paper roll to push away any paper that may be causing an obstruction.
- Fold the pointed end of the other roll lengthways (so it becomes pointier).
- If that doesn't help: cut the pointed end so that it is pointier.

If it is still not working, position the two ends over each other and continue to weave—the next round of weaving will secure it.

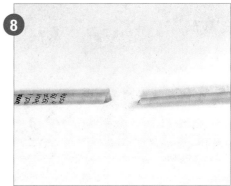

Tip

Your hands will get dirty when making the rolls and weaving with them—the ink from the paper will color your fingertips gray to black. Don't worry. These inks are not hazardous and can be washed away with soap and water without leaving any stains.

It's important to store the rolls so that the ends don't get bent. If you can protect the ends, you'll hardly have any problems when it comes to inserting the rolls into each other.

2.2 Time required

You should plan just under one minute per roll (including cutting the paper strips). Therefore, you can easily make over 60 rolls in an hour.

2.3 Different lengths

You'll need short paper rolls for some projects. In such cases, simply cut the paper strips to the desired length and then make the rolls. Unfortunately, cutting long rolls to create shorter ones doesn't work too well because the rolls are stuck together with glue in one position, and the end unwinds after a part has been cut off.

For very large objects, you sometimes need very long rolls. If you simply insert one roll into another, the weave will have a weak point because the point of connection may be unstable. Glue alone does not provide the necessary hold. Therefore, I recommend pushing a small piece of florist's wire into the pointed end of a paper roll, coating the connection point with glue and then inserting it into the funnel-shaped end of the paper roll (figs. 10–11).

2.4 Different thicknesses

To stabilize the corners of square or rectangular baskets, use particularly thick and stable stakes. To make such rolls, you can simply use broader strips. However, sometimes you'll need very thin and flexible rolls (e.g., to make a basket handle). For this purpose, make paper rolls from strips that are approximately 2.75 inches wide.

2.5 Stabilize with wire

To create particularly stable yet simultaneously flexible rolls, you can use florist's wire. Carefully straighten the wire (pull it over the edge of a table or between your fingernails to smooth it). Then push it into the roll from the funnel-shaped end. For this method to work, the first couple of centimeters of the wire must be completely straight. Cut off any projecting wire. You should bend back the ends of the wire so that you do not injure yourself while weaving. Push the bent-back end into the roll (figs. 12–13).

PRACTICAL TIP: Do you think you don't have the time to make paper rolls? I make the rolls while I'm on the phone, watching a movie, or enjoying my morning coffee, or when I'm helping my young daughter with her homework. And the pile of rolls grows as if by magic.

DICTIONARY CORNER: *I simply call my homemade paper rolls "rolls." The rolls that give the weave its form like a skeleton are called "stakes" (rectangular baskets) or "spokes" (circular baskets). The paper rolls that are woven around the stakes or spokes are called "weavers" (fig. 14).*

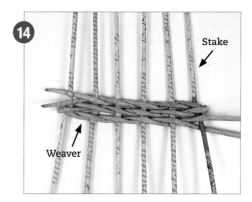

Stake

Weaver

3. The Weaving Techniques

3.1 Weaving with one weaver

The principle is easy: an individual paper roll is led alternately in front and behind the stakes (figs. 1–2). This technique requires an uneven number of stakes so that the next round always begins on the opposite side to the previous round. The finished weave is not quite as stable as the technique that uses two weavers.

3.2 Weaving with two weavers

Weaving with two weavers is the most important method for weaving with paper. The two weavers are wound over each other like twine and then worked around the stakes (fig. 3). In the beginning, a chaotic weave could easily develop if you do not realize the following: there are essentially two options for moving the two weavers around the next stake and twining them together (figs. 4–5). If you change the weaving technique halfway through, then the finished weave looks uneven. However, if you stick to one of the options, then the weave will be even from the beginning.

Experiment to discover which finger movements and which direction are the most comfortable for you when weaving.

For my favorite technique, I always work from right to left (clockwise) where possible. I insert two rolls into two spaces next to each other (i.e., to the right and left of a stake). The long ends of the paper rolls are facing outward (fig. 6). (The short inward-facing ends can be cut off once the weave is completed.)

Use your right hand to hold both weavers to the stake (fig. 8). Now the index finger on your right hand pushes the back weaver forward and down-

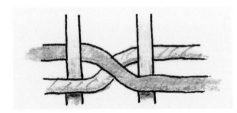

Weaving method 1: Illustration for fig. 4

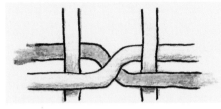

Weaving method 2: Illustration for fig. 5

ward, while your right thumb pushes the front weaver backward and upward (fig. 9). This technique corresponds to weaving method 1.

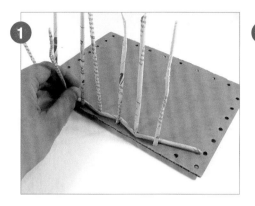

Tip

You can bend a paper roll in half and place it around the first stake. The two ends of this first paper roll then become the first two weavers. This start is a little thicker and more noticeable than the start with two paper rolls; however, it is easier (fig. 7).

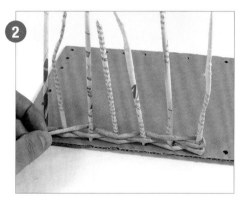

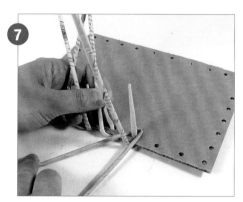

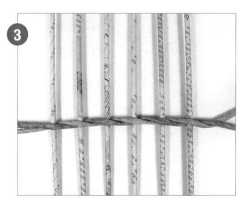

When using this method, your right hand makes a slight movement, like screwing a lid on a bottle.

Use your left hand to bend the stake on the left to the side and position it between the two weavers. Press the weavers firmly around the stake (figs. 10–11).

Then move your right hand a stake farther to the left, while your left hand holds the weavers if required. Your right index finger is now resting on the back weaver again, and your thumb is on the front weaver (fig. 12).

Repeat these steps. If you practice these movements right from the beginning and don't vary them, you'll achieve a beautiful weave from your very first basket. When weaving, always forcefully pack the already woven basket sides downward. Pay attention that you do not work too tightly and thus pull the weave together, unless you intend to have a shape that narrows toward the top. You should also not work too loosely because it will cause the basket to become wider at the top.

While weaving, keep checking the direction of the stakes. If the stakes are pointing inward, it could be an indication that you are weaving too tightly. If the stakes are pointing outward, then the weave may be too loose.

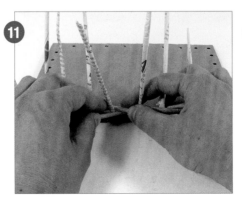

Why not try weighing down the base of the basket? Books, bags of sugar or flour, a large stone, a sack of bird sand, and similar are suitable for this purpose. It often makes weaving a lot easier.

3.3 Crossover pattern

There are innumerable decorative weaving techniques. As an example, I'll show you the crossover pattern. This pattern has very different appearances depending on the colors you choose and whether your basket has an even (fig. 13) or odd (fig. 14) number of stakes or spokes. In this method, you work with four weavers at the same time: two weavers are worked together in front and behind the stakes ("parallel weavers") (fig. 15), and two weavers ("crossover weavers") (fig. 16) are worked around the parallel weavers in a cross pattern.

If the two parallel weavers are behind the stake, then the two crossover weavers are crossed in front of this stake. If the parallel weavers are in front of the stake, then the crossover weaves are worked above and below behind the stake. Repeat these two steps alternately (figs. 17–20).

4. Shaping

If you want to create a shape that opens toward the top, you should always forcefully bend the stakes outward while weaving and imagine that you are placing the round you are working on outside the round below. It needs some practice to achieve the shape that you want.

If you want to use a form to weave around in order to create a shape that greatly widens, you should turn the form upside down and place your weaving on it. Weigh it down and weave from top to bottom. In doing so, the stakes are bent; however, that does not cause any problems (see "Source of Vitamins—A Fruit Bowl," p. 90).

At some point, the space between the stakes will become too big due to the increased diameter. That also happens when weaving a large basket base. In these cases, additional stakes must be inserted.

Inserting stakes

You can insert one or two stakes by weaving in an additional folded paper roll between two stakes.
• Fold the roll at one end to insert it as an individual stake (figs. 5–6).
• Fold the roll in half to get two stakes, which you initially weave as one (figs. 7–9). You can divide them later, when the diameter of the basket has considerably grown (fig. 10).

Tip

You can insert stakes in the space between stakes, in every second space or, for example, just in four places symmetrically distributed around the basket. The wider the shape becomes, the more stakes you need to insert.

Tip

To achieve a very precise and cleanly worked shape, you can place a suitable container (or for square shapes, a box) in your basket and weave closely around it. You may have to change your weaving technique slightly to do so (figs. 1–4). It's very helpful to heavily weigh down the container or box.

5. The Basket Bases

5.1 Bases made of cardboard

Cardboard is wonderfully suited as a basket base for smaller projects. You can also create larger bases from thicker and more stable chip board, which you can buy in various thicknesses. The advantages of a cardboard base are obvious—it can be simply and quickly made, and it is closed so nothing can fall through it.

There are several methods of attaching the stakes to a cardboard base.

Glue/stapling

The ends of the stakes are glued (½ to 1 inch from the edge) (fig. 1) or stapled (fig. 2) along the edge of the cardboard. Glue a second piece of cardboard of the same size over the first piece (fig. 3) to hide the glue/staples. Glue sticks or liquid glues are suitable options. Stapling creates the most-stable joins. Fold the stakes upward and start weaving.

Punching holes in the base

Along the edge of the base, punch holes at equal intervals (using a punch or hole punch with a 0.2-inch diameter). The distance between the holes (from hole center to hole center) should be ½ to 1 inch; the distance from the hole center to the base edge should be approximately 0.2 to 0.5 inches.

There are two methods for inserting the stakes

1. **For particularly long stakes:** Insert approximately 2 inches of the prepared roll from below through the hole and bend the rest of the stake upward on the outside (fig. 4). With this method, you must always weave the short stake ends into the first row of the weave. First insert a few stakes and start weaving so that these stakes can no longer slip out of the holes. Little by little, add further stakes and in this way gradually work around the basket base (fig. 5).

2. **For shorter stakes:** Push a stake from above through a hole and then pull it up from below through the neighboring hole. Pull the end of the paper roll until both stakes are of equal length (fig. 6).

5.2 Wooden bases

If you need more stability, a wooden base is a good option (e.g., from plywood). You can buy these bases or make one yourself (distance from hole center to hole center: ½ to 1 inch; distance from edge to hole center: 0.2–0.4 inches; drill bit size: 5 mm). The stakes are inserted in the same way as with a punched cardboard base (see also figs. 4–6).

5.3 Woven bases

Not only is creating a woven surface useful for basket bases—you can also use them to put under pots, as table mats, or as seat pads (see p. 75).

Tip

It is generally advisable to not fully pull up the stakes in the first couple of rounds. It stops the paper base from being seen from outside and gives the basket a more pleasing appearance (figs. 7–8).

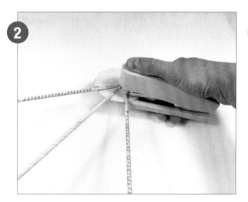

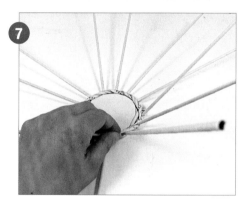

Tip

You can buy ready-made wooden basket bases that are intended for wicker work. However, the holes have a very small diameter of just 3 mm. If you have a drill, you can increase the size to 5 mm. If not, make very tightly rolled paper rolls so that the pointed ends can be pushed a few centimeters through the small holes.

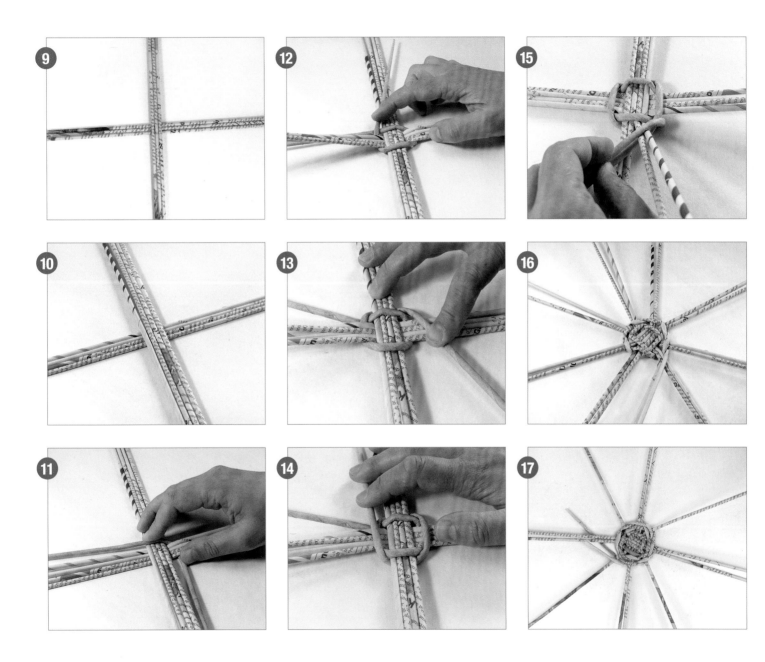

Round bases

There are very many different methods to make a round basket base. I'll show you the most common. First, you need a basic frame made of crossed paper rolls, which I call the spoke cross. The spokes for the basket emerge from the spoke cross. Select the number of crossed paper rolls depending on the size of the

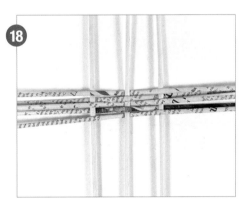

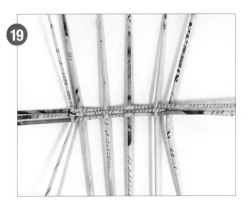

planned base. For bases whose diameter is to be less than 4 inches, a spoke cross of 3+3 spokes is enough (fig. 9). For larger bases, you will need 4+4 spokes (fig. 10).

Either way, you hold the spoke cross in place with a paper roll by weaving it over and under the bundle of spokes (figs. 11–14). After two times around, the ends of the paper roll meet again, and together they become the two weavers (fig. 15).

Pay attention to ensure that you weave in your usual weave direction (for me, it is clockwise). At first, you don't weave around each spoke on its own but combine them into a bundle. For 4+4 spokes, you should always initially weave around groups of two (fig. 16); for 3+3, you weave alternately around a group of 2 and a single spoke (fig. 17).

Continue to work in this way until you see that there's enough space between the spokes for another spoke. Then separate the pairs of spokes, and in the subsequent rounds, weave around each spoke individually.

If you are making a very large basket base, after some time the distance between the spokes will be too big. You should then insert additional spokes (see p. 18).

"When I weave a basket base, large holes appear in the weave"

When weaving a basket base, you must work very tightly—which takes some practice. You should not really let go of the weavers while you are working. If you have to do so, hold your place with a peg. The problem may also occur if you are working on round or oval bases with too many spokes. At first, weave around two spokes as one and do not separate them too soon. Only once the spaces between the spokes are big enough for an additional spoke to be positioned there without any problem should you separate the spokes (or insert new spokes).

Oval bases

You also start oval bases with a spoke cross that is planned according to the desired size of the basket base (e.g., with 3+4 or with 7+3 spokes) (figs. 8–19).

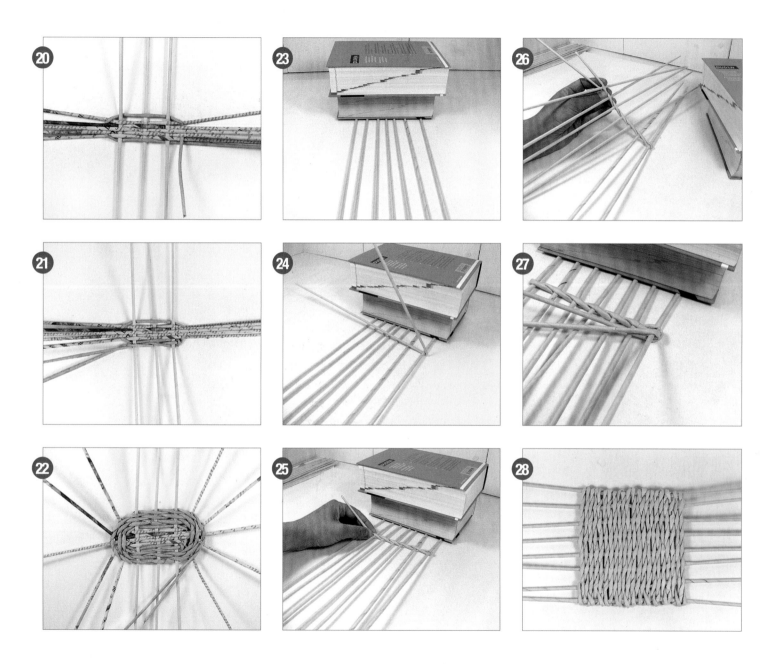

Just like with round basket bases, you use a paper roll to weave around this spoke cross and fix it in place as follows (fig. 20): when the beginning and end of the (possibly extended) paper roll meet again, you will have two weavers, with which you can weave. Work in your usual weave direction (figs. 21–22). Sometimes, you should still weave around spoke pairs together (effectively as a single spoke) and then separate them only later, once the basket base has become bigger.

Square and rectangular bases

Place the stakes on a table next to each other at a distance of approximately ½ to 1 inch. The two outer stakes determine the width of your basket base. Place a couple of heavy books on the farthest ends of the stakes or stick them to the table with masking tape that can later be removed (fig. 23). Then start to weave around the stakes (figs. 24–25).

Once you have woven around the final stake, fold the weaver around it. Now you can either work backward or turn the whole base around, secure in place with books (or masking tape) again, and continue to weave (figs. 26–27). Continue in this way until the base has reached the desired size (fig. 28). Finally, pull a little on the opposite ends of the stakes until they protrude at equal lengths on both sides.

5.4 Connecting the woven basket base to basket side

There are three options:

1. You can simply upset the basket by folding the stakes or spokes from the base upward and using them to weave the basket sides (fig. 29). For smaller items, that works well because the stakes or spokes are long enough anyway. For larger items, you will have to extend the stakes or spokes (see p. 13, 2.3).

(see p. 13, 2.3)

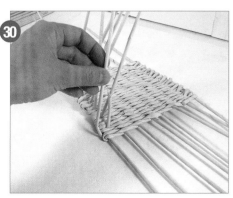

Tip

The phenomenon of edges curving upward on a basket base often occurs when making bases. Fortunately, the weave is very flexible—it can sometimes even be corrected while weaving if you occasionally bend and push it into the correct shape. If that isn't enough, you can place the weave under a pile of books for a couple of hours. In a finished basket, you can place a couple of bags of flour or similar in it overnight to give the curved base the correct shape.

2. Alternatively, you can completely finish the basket base by working a normal basket rim (see p. 26).
Then you continue in the same way as for a paper or wooden base: in each space, there is a hole between the base stakes or spokes through which the stakes or spokes for the basket side can be inserted (see p. 20).

3. The third option is a combination of the first two: bend the remaining stake ends of the basket upward, but at the same time insert a new stake or spoke next to each one. When weaving, you work the new and old stakes or spokes as one. When the stake from the basket base ends, you still have the newly inserted stake or spoke to continue your weaving and to finish off with a rim (fig. 30).

6. The Rims

There are many different rim techniques that you can use, depending on requirements and your taste.

6.1 Simple tucked rim

For this way of finishing off, you tuck each stake or spoke into the "opening" from which the next stake or spoke emerges. To do so, shorten the stakes or spokes to the **distance to the next stake or spoke plus approximately ¾–1½ inches** by cutting the end diagonally. A narrow, flat instrument (e.g., a letter opener, blunt scissors, or a thin knife) is helpful for tucking in the stake or spoke into the opening next to it (fig. 1). Turn the tool 90 degrees (fig. 2), allowing the slit to open somewhat and the stake or spoke to be more easily inserted (fig. 3). If any ends of the weavers are still protruding, cut them off once the rim is completed.

6.2 Loop rim

For this rim, the ends of the stakes or spokes should be a little longer than for the simple tucked rim: about **twice the distance to the next stake or spoke plus 1 inch.** Each stake or spoke is wrapped around the next one from behind and then inserted back in the opening it came from (figs. 4–5).

6.3 Basket weave rim

For this rim, you need a remaining stake or spoke length of at least **twice the distance to the next stake plus 1½ inches.** First fold all the stakes or spokes behind the one to the right of them, so that all the stakes or spokes are pointing outward like rays of sun (fig. 6). The final stake or spoke is pushed from behind through the loop that the first folded stake or spoke forms (figs. 7–8). Now push the outward-pointing ends through the loops on the right side (fig. 9). Individually pull each stake or spoke tight and check the appearance of the rim (fig. 10). If you are happy with it, cut off any protruding stakes or spokes, which should be pointing inward, and any remaining ends of the weaver (not too closely)—voilà!

Tip

Sometimes, the tucked ends slip out of the weave. The stake or spoke ends can be easily secured with a drop of superglue.

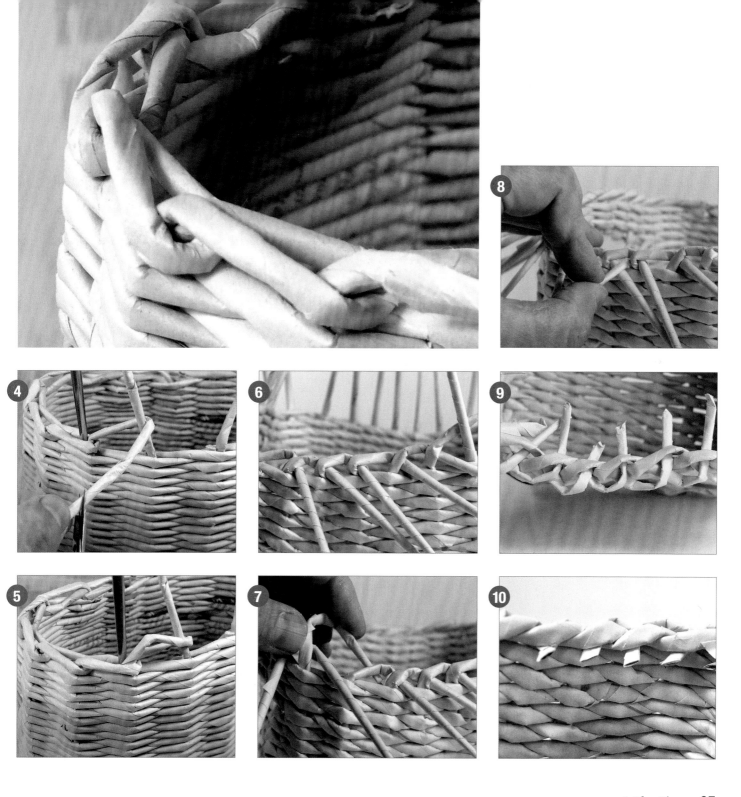

7. The Handles

There are various methods to add a handle to your basket.

7.1 Inserted handles

You should first consider what purpose the inserted handles should fulfill on the finished basket: Are they supposed to be a decorative element for a small basket, will they have to carry heavy loads, or should they be stable enough to really withstand wear and tear? Your decision determines the properties of the inside of the handle. Depending on what loads they should carry, you will need two to five paper rolls. If you want to achieve a very high level of dependability, you can also strengthen the paper rolls with wire (see p. 13). Also, the way in which you join the handle to the basket has an influence on their later stability: in most cases, it is enough to simply insert the handle into the basket weave.

Think about how big the handle should be so that you can use it with ease later. Fold both ends of the paper rolls intended for the handle so that you can make a suitable handle from the middle part.

The folded ends must be at least 3–4 inches long. Now, find a suitable place in the basket side to insert your handle (fig. 2). If you want to insert two handles, ensure they are positioned symmetrically. Push one side of your prepared handle through the weave of the basket and fold the ends upward so that you can hold them together with the handle. To make the work easier, you can hold the end of the handle in place with a peg or masking tape (fig. 3).

Now, the handle needs to be covered. I would like to show you two methods to do this.

Wrapping

Attach (if necessary, using glue) a paper roll into the opening of a stake or spoke, close to where the handle joins the basket, and wrap it around the handle (fig. 4). When you attach a new roll, use glue to stick it into the previous roll. Once the handle has been more than half wrapped, insert the second end of the handle into the basket weave, bend the ends upward, and wrap these ends too (fig. 5). Finally, insert the end of the paper roll into the opening of the stake or spoke.

If necessary, shorten the roll a little and trim into a point. It is best to secure it with glue.

Knotting

I think it's very pretty to tie decorative knots around the handle. To do so, you need a couple of very thin paper rolls (roll approximately 2½-inch-wide strips of newspaper or similar). The rolls must be so thin that they have the flexibility of a ribbon. They have to be made very carefully and precisely and have well-pointed ends; otherwise you can't join them.

For the knotting technique, you should attach the end of the thin paper rolls in the opening of a stake or spoke very close to where the handle joints the basket (using glue if necessary).

Tip

If you need the handle to carry a heavy weight, you should weave in an additional stake or spoke into the basket at the start and work it as part of the handle (fig. 1).

1

2

3

4

Press your fingers together and pull the paper roll through them to almost the end—doing so makes them more flexible. However, you shouldn't press the funnel-shaped end, so that you can later insert the next roll into it. Tie knots around the handle: use the thin paper roll to make a small loop close to the handle (fig. 6), wrap the end around the handle and through the loop (fig. 7), and carefully pull it tight (fig. 8). Now repeat the steps (figs. 9–11). Be particularly careful when attaching the next roll. Put a little glue on the pointed roll tip and insert it into the other end of the roll and secure the joint with a peg (pay attention so that the peg does not accidentally become glued to the paper roll).

Tip

Well-used handles should be given a coat of protective varnish—otherwise they can quickly appear tatty. Don't be afraid to add several coats of varnish! If the handle eventually looks worn, you can simply replace it with a new one.

If you want to attach two handles to your basket, work alternately on each handle; continue working on one handle while the glue is drying on the other. Once it's dry, continue working extremely carefully. You should not exert much pressure on the join but form the knots through pushing and pressing. Once the join has been worked in, you can work as usual with some pressure. Now and again, push the knots together so that the handle is well covered in knots. Remember to attach the other side of the handle into the basket and knot around the fold-ed-up ends of the paper rolls. Finally, secure the end of the thin paper roll in the basket side near to the handle.

7.2 Handles within the weave

A very beautiful and simple way to form a handle is to work it in while weaving. A few inches from the planned basket rim, work four neighboring stakes or spokes into a simple tucked rim (see p. 26 and fig. 12). In the next round of weaving, insert four new stakes or spokes; if needed, hold in place with pegs until you get to the next round (fig. 13). The more stakes or spokes you insert, the bigger the handle. After about four rows when the basket rim is reached, cut off one stake or spoke per pair on the handle (fig. 14) and work a rim.

12

13

14

7.3 Handles within the weave and a straight rim

If you want a straight rim, you can work in holes for the handles. Choose where the handle should be, and work the stakes or spokes into a rim in the same manner as before with the simple handle within the weave. Pass a weaver around the stake or spoke that is to form the side of the hole, and start weaving in the opposite direction (fig. 15). Pay attention to maintaining the even appearance of your basket side when you are working backward (e.g., don't accidentally twine the weavers together; see p. 14). Look at the appearance of the weave to that point and try to replicate it "backward." If your basket is to have two handles, weave to the position of the handle hole on the opposite side, pass the weaver around the stake or spoke that is to form the side of the hole, and then weave forward to the first hole. Continue in this way until you have woven around four rows (fig. 16). Now weave four rows on the other side, using a new weaver (fig. 17), and simply cut it off after four rows. Use the other weaver to weave over the gap and form the handle holes. Insert a corresponding number of stakes or spokes above the gap and between the weavers (fig. 18), then continue to weave as normal.

Tip

If you don't want to weave the stakes or spokes on the bottom of the handle hole into a rim, you can make use of them farther up. It looks particularly decorative if you cross over the stakes or spokes (fig. 19).

8. Coloring and Protective Coating

8.1 Using the color of the paper

First, I'd like to invite you to do a small experiment for which you need a sheet of printing paper. Cut the paper length-ways and place the strips crossways in front of you on the table. Then color in two edges (approximately ½ inch) of the paper, as shown in fig. 1, with a high-lighter or pencil. Now turn the paper over as shown in fig. 2 (I have shaded the area on the back that was colored), and roll the paper strips as normal on a skewer. Start from the lower left corner (figs. 3–4). Now, the roll should be almost completely the color of the colored edges (fig. 5). If you want to experiment with the colors of the rolls, you also need to know this fact: it is only these two edges of the paper strip that later define the color of the paper roll.

You can make use of it in two ways: you can create rolls that are completely white if you use the unprinted margin of a newspaper, or you can create particularly colorful rolls if you ensure that the relevant edges of your strip are very colorful.

Each strip of paper offers you four options to vary the colors.

White rolls

In many cases, white paper rolls are useful; for example, if you want to weave a white basket or combine white weaving with a colored element. The great thing is that you do not need to plunder your store of printer paper, but you can make white paper rolls from completely normal sheets of newspaper, without using any additional color (fig. 6).

Colored rolls

You can make a store of colorful paper rolls from particularly colorful catalogs or newspapers (fig. 7). If you sort these rolls according to color, you can achieve beautiful effects!

8.2 Acrylic paint

Painting finished baskets

Acrylic paint is well suited for adding color to a finished basket. It adheres particularly well to normal newspaper. You can also thin the acrylic paint a little to achieve a somewhat glazed and paler effect. Do a color test on a newspaper before painting. Synthetic-bristle brushes are well suited for painting. To get the paint completely in the weave, hold the brush at a 90° angle to the weave and press the brush with small movements into the cracks and crevices of the basket surface. Also paint the basket in the direction of the weave.

Prepainting the rolls

Sometimes, it makes sense to prepaint the paper rolls; for example, if you want to work a colored pattern or if you have a beautiful wooden base that you don't want to get drips on. When you want to paint a lot of rolls, it's advisable to dunk them in a dye bath. Some people use egg dyes, or they color the water with crepe paper for the dye bath. I found that acrylic paints worked best because I can mix them to the exact color that I want. The more you thin the acrylic paint, the paler the color of the paper will be (a rough recipe is 1 tablespoon of acrylic paint to 1 cup of water). First, mix the paste-like paint with a little water until it is smooth, and then continue thinning it so that the dye bath is not lumpy (with a cup of the

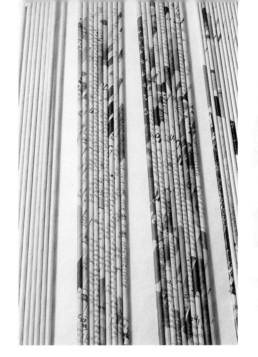

Tip

Since newspaper paper contains wood fibers, it darkens in the same way as wood. Over time, the white paper turns yellow. If you want your weaving to remain white permanently, then paint a white glaze on it (e.g., from thinned white acrylic paint).

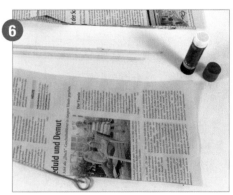

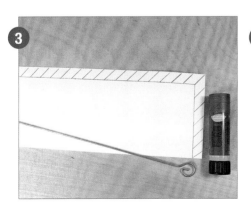

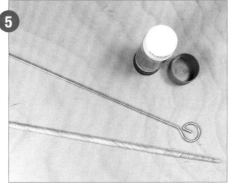

To dip the rolls, you need a container where the ends of the rolls do not touch the edges. Instead of using a garbage bag, you could also use a plastic window box to dip the rolls. (Of course, it shouldn't have any holes in it.)

paint-water mixture, you can dye 100 to 150 rolls). It's sensible to do a color test on the newspaper before you dye the rolls (fig. 8). First, cover the table with a thick layer of newspaper. Then form a large, sturdy garbage bag into a long, thin bath, pour the paint-water mix into it, and add the rolls (fig. 9). For the next part, you should wear plastic gloves. Carefully move the rolls in the bath (fig. 10). Sometimes, the glue comes unstuck on the rolls when dunking them in the water-paint mixture. Simply push these bits back into place—the wet rolls should keep their shape.

Allow the dyed rolls to drip over the bath and then leave them to dry on an old cooling rack (fig. 11) or over an open cardboard box (fig. 12). While they are drying, occasionally check that the rolls aren't sticking together, and pull them apart if they do. To get rid of the remaining paint from the garbage bag, cut a hole in the bottom of the sack and pour it into a jam jar (fig. 13).

I keep the leftover dye in case I need more rolls than I thought or if I want to cover over any spots on the finished basket. You can seal the hole in the bag with a clip or a rubber band so you can use it again (fig. 14).

Stenciling

On large woven surfaces, stenciled patterns also look very decorative. To do so, you need a stencil made of newspaper.

Use pins to carefully attach the sheet of paper to the basket. The edge of the design must always be very close to the basket. It is better to use a few too many pins than not enough! Put some acrylic paint (emulsion / color varnish / wood varnish) into a jam jar lid or an old saucer and dip a synthetic-bristle

Tip

With dyed rolls, the ends often stick a little, which can lead to difficulties in inserting them into each other to make weavers. If you need help with that, then check out the tips on p. 10.

brush in it so that the bristles take on the color but look very dry.

Dab or stroke the paint over the prepared stencil opening (fig. 15) and remember to move the brush in the direction of the weave. Let the paint dry and only then remove the stencil (fig. 16). If necessary, you can correct the shape with a fine brush.

Tip

If you have never used a stencil, you should practice the technique on a newspaper. For small shapes or for straight lines, you can also use masking tape (fig. 17).

PRACTICAL TIP: Spray paint is very well suited for painting basket weave because the spray gets into all the nooks and crannies. Two coats of spray paint are generally required for the basket to have an even color. For stenciling, you have to be careful with spray paint because it may run under the stencil. It is an absolute must to test the paint in advance.

8.3 Sealing and protecting

To protect baskets from wear, dirt, or water droplets, you can use a selection of protective varnishes. Decoupage varnish or other varnishes with a water base give a slight shine and protect well. However, they also slightly change the color of the weave—it turns a little darker and has a slight yellow tinge. I particularly like using them on areas that are heavily used, such as handles. Spray varnishes with solvents sometimes smell unpleasant, but they do not change the color as much.

8.4 Food-safe paint/varnish

If you weave a basket that may later be used for food, you should think about how food-safe the basket surface will be. In this case, acrylic paint and decoupage varnish are not suitable, nor is untreated newspaper. For example, for a fruit basket, I use a paint or varnish that is suitable for children's toys.

8.5 Wood varnish

Weave that has been treated with a wood varnish appears almost like weave made from basket willow, wicker, or other natural materials, depending on the color. The result is very shiny. If you use a very dark varnish, it does not matter about print on the paper because the varnish covers all colors—only red occasionally shines through. If you want to use a light-colored varnish, then you should make white rolls unless you want the print with letters or colors to be visible.

When selecting the varnish, remember that the color cards generally show what the varnish will look like on wood. It could therefore be slightly lighter when you paint it onto a white weave. You should always test the color on a piece of newspaper before you paint your finished basket!

I personally like to work with wood paint (fig. 18). It can be bought in small pots, smells only a little, and goes on very well. Furthermore, they are available in different, even very colorful shades and can be mixed together.

Driftwood, Beech, Walnut, Pine, Cedar, Oak, and Rosewood

Projects

You can design a wide variety of baskets using the various elements that have been described in the instruction section. The projects that I show here are primarily to be used as a source of inspiration for your own projects. There are so many design options, especially when using color.

Basic Basket – Your First Project

Technical difficulty ★ Time required ★ Color ★

If you've never woven a basket, you should first try this practical little basket. You'll learn the most-important basic techniques, and after 90 minutes to two hours, you will be holding your first self-woven artwork in your hands!

TOOLS AND MATERIALS

- Two cardboard circles (3-inch diameter)
- 20 long rolls of newspaper (approximately 20 inches long), 12 short rolls (approximately 10 inches long)
- Scissors
- A stick of glue or a good liquid glue

IMPORTANT INFO

- "Rolls of newspaper" are always made as described in the instructions on p. 10. They are approximately 20 inches long (the number of rolls must be correspondingly increased if the rolls are shorter or reduced if the rolls are longer).
- I made "short rolls" from halved newspaper strips (i.e., they are approximately 10 inches long).

HOW TO

1. Stick the 12 short paper rolls on the cardboard circle so that they look like rays of sun and are an equal distance apart, similar to the numbers on a clock (see fig. 1 on p. 21). The glued rolls will form the basic framework for your basket. You call them "spokes" on circular or oval baskets and "stakes" on square or rectangular baskets. Use liquid glue to stick the second circle on top of them, so that the ends of the spokes are no longer visible (see fig. 3 on p. 21). Press together and wait for the glue to dry.

2. Now you can start the actual weaving. Carefully read the instructions for "weaving with two weavers" from p. 14 onward, and work with uniform hand movements. When there are only a few inches of a weaver left, take the next one and gently push it into the end of the weaver with a slight turning movement (see. p. 13). Work in a spiral upward and keep forcefully packing the sides downward.

3. When the little basket has reached its intended height (at the latest, when the spokes are still protruding by 3 inches), stop weaving. You can simply cut off the ends of the weavers. Now for the rim. On page 26, you can see several options for weaving rims. Select one that you like. I used a basket weave rim.

Congratulations, you have completed your first basket! Are you surprised at the stability and strength of a weave made from normal paper? Do you want to make more practical things from paper rolls? Then start weaving your next project!

VARIATIONS

- What about a basket made of old magazines? Or a combination of white newspaper rolls and colorful rolls from advertising leaflets (see p. 34)?

- You can make a larger base in any shape (round, oval, square) and weave higher basket sides. Or make a small tray with very low basket sides.

- If you want, you can give your newspaper basket a colorful style with wood varnish or acrylic paint.

- Why not try the square basket on p. 78? You can replace the woven base with a square paper base.

Starring Role – A Tray

Technical difficulty ★ Time required ★ ★ Coloring ★ ★

This tray is not difficult to make, and it's very practical.
The base provides a lot of space for you to let your creative juices flow. I chose some
lettering that shows everyone that paper plays a starring role in this tray.

TOOLS AND MATERIALS

- A plywood base, approximately 19 x 12 inches holes around the edges (see p. 20)
- White acrylic paint and brush
- Approximately 100 white and printed newspaper rolls (see p. 34); approximately 60 short rolls as stakes
- 4 newspaper rolls strengthened with wire (see p. 13) for the handles
- For the lettering in the center: a permanent marker with a fine tip in black, clear varnish and brush, a printed template (download from my website, www.pirlipause.de), pencils, scissors, newspaper, masking tape. (Note: the words in the template are German for "Starring Role," a bit of a pun for the paper rolls you use.)
- 4 thick felt furniture pads

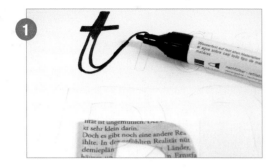

HOW TO

1. Paint the plywood base with white acrylic paint. If it doesn't cover properly, give it a second coat. Ensure that the surface is smooth.

2. Now for the lettering! Use a pencil to carefully sketch the lines of your lettering on a template (press a little when writing). Center the sheet right in the middle on the painted white base. The side with the pencil on should be facing down. Secure it with glue that can be removed later. Carefully use a pencil to redraw all the lines on the back of the sheet. When you remove the sheet, the writing should be visible and the correct way around on the base.

3. You'll also need the template to help cut out the word "rolle" out of newspaper. Place the sheet on a newspaper (ensure that is a section of the paper that consists purely of text) and trace the letters onto the newspaper. Cut out the letters and use a glue stick to stick them in the desired place on the base.

4. Use the permanent marker to color the word "tragende" and allow it to dry (fig. 1). Then paint the tray with a coat of thinned white acrylic paint. Once the acrylic paint has dried, use a brush to paint the whole base with a clear varnish.

5. Attach the short rolls as stakes to the tray base (see figs. 4–5 on p. 21). In the four holes where the handle is to be located, insert one stake as well as one of the long, wire-strengthened paper rolls (see tip on p. 28). The two ends of this long stake should protrude upward at an equal height. Weave all the stakes in this hole as one single thick stake.

6. For my tray, I wove a striped pattern of white and printed paper rolls. The first three rounds were completely white rounds, then came three rounds with newspaper print, and finally, white rolls again. When weaving the corners, pay particular attention that the shape is well formed. Bend and press everything into the correct position.

7. Once the tray sides have reached the desired height, work a basket weave rim (see p. 26). To do this, the stakes must still be at least 3½ inches long. However, at the handle, you weave in only the short stakes. The wire-strengthened stakes remain unworked for the time being (fig. 2).

8. Now it is time for the handles. Shape the handles from the protruding ends of the wire-strengthened paper rolls (fig. 3) and hold in place with pegs or masking tape. Attach a new paper roll at the bottom of each handle and wrap it evenly around the arches (see p. 28)—you remove the pegs one by one as you work. If you used masking tape, you should wrap the paper roll around it so that you can no longer see it (fig. 4).

9. If you want to keep your tray from turning yellow over time, you can give it a coat of thinned white acrylic paint (see tip on p. 35). Finally, paint a varnish onto the weave (don't be too sparing, especially on the handles). The varnish protects the tray against damp and the handles from becoming worn.

10. To ensure that the paper stakes on the bottom of the tray do not become worn, even with a lot of use, stick furniture felt pads under all four corners.

Tip

If you are unable to get hold of a cut board and put holes in it, you can use two pieces of stable cardboard of the same size (e.g., gray board with a thickness of 2.7 mm) and stick the stakes between the cardboard, using a good glue. However, the handles must be attached to the paper base by using four holes.

A Flowery Box on the Shelf

Technical difficulty ★ Time required ★ ★ ★ Coloring ★ ★

You can quickly tidy up your shelf with a square or
rectangular basket. If you then embroider your box,
it becomes a wonderful eye-catcher!

TOOLS AND MATERIALS

- A board that has holes around the edges (MDF
  board, plywood) (see p. 20) or thick cardboard
  with holes around the edges (e.g., gray cardboard; see p. 20) in the correct size
- Paper rolls made of newspaper (the amount
  depends on the size of the basket base and on
  the height of the basket). My basket is 10
  inches wide and 7½ inches high, and for this
  size, I needed 150 to 200 rolls.
- White glaze (e.g., made of thinned white acrylic
  paint) and a brush
- Raffia in various colors and a large embroidery
  needle
- 4 felt furniture pads

HOW TO

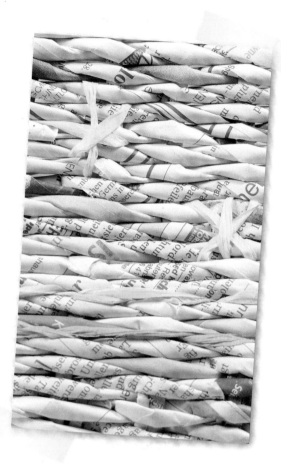

1. Insert the stakes one by one into the holes in the basket base and immediately weave around them, using two weavers (see figs. 4–5 on p. 21).

2. Now continue to weave until you get to approximately 3 inches below the intended basket rim. Pay particular attention to the shaping at the corners, because corners have a tendency to lean inward!

3. Now for the handle holes (see p. 33). In my case, I worked only one handle hole because my shelf has a back. Weave four rows back and forth from one side of the handle hole to the other.

4. Close the handle hole in the manner described on p. 33; weave a couple more rounds and then work a basket weave rim (see p. 26).

5. If you want to prevent your basket from turning yellow over time, paint it with thinned white acrylic paint.

6. Finally, decorate your basket with colorful flowers, using the raffia and the embroidery needle. Or sew stripes or stars to it. Let your imagination run wild.

7. Under all four corners of the basket, stick the thick felt furniture pads.

Tip

Fully use the depth and height of your shelf. I find the following calculation works perfectly: depth of the basket base = depth of shelf base minus ¾–1 inch.

Desk Organizer

Technical difficulty ★ Time required ★ ★ ★ Coloring ★ ★ ★

If you want to tidy up your office, this project could be just right for you.
It's not difficult in terms of technique, but you'll need a little perseverance.
Afterward, you will be rewarded with a homemade A4 desk organizer.

TOOLS AND MATERIALS

- 3 plywood bases or thick cardboard bases of 13 x 10 inches, with equally spaced holes on three sides. The holes should have a minimum diameter of 2 inches; 2½ inches would be better. (See p. 13.)
- A couple of wooden toothpicks
- Approximately 140 to 150 precolored rolls made of newspaper (see p. 34); don't throw away the leftover paint
- Optional: 1 or 2 matching wooden drawers made of wood or cardboard

HOW TO

1. Position the first base in front of you so that the side without the holes is facing you. Start inserting the stakes from the left (see p. 20). Use a paper roll folded in half as the first two weavers (see tip on p. 15).

2. To stabilize the four corners and ensure that they stand straight, you can insert two toothpicks in the same hole as the corners stakes and incorporate them in the weaving.

3. Bend the weavers around the final stake when you are finished with the first row of weaving, then continue to weave backward. Weaving backward is initially very strange—be careful that the appearance of the weave is the same as the previous row (see p. 14).

4. If you want to insert a drawer, continue weaving until it is high enough for the drawer to fit easily. The edge of the weave should be just higher than the drawer.

5. Now add the next wooden base (fig. 1). This can be a little tricky. It should work a little easier if you cut the tips of the stakes into a point. Don't be afraid to fold and bend the stakes; otherwise, the base will not go on. Start pushing the stakes on one side through the holes and then work around the rest of the base. Push the base gradually downward by pulling the stakes.

6. Now weave the sides for the middle level to the desired height and add the second wooden base.

7. Work on the sides for the upper level and finish it off with a basket weave rim (see p. 26). So that the tray appears symmetrical from the front, I have worked the rim on both sides from the front to the back (fig. 2). Where the two rims meet, you will have to improvise a little. Work symmetrically. If one stake is left over, simply tuck it back into the weave (figs. 3–4).

8. Finally, paint your cutoff stake ends with the leftover paint (fig. 5).

Tip

Remember the way you wrapped the weavers around the final stake in the first row, and do it in the same way in the following rows. It makes the edges look the same on both sides (see below).

Decorative Paper Lamps

Technical difficulty ★ ★   Time required ★   Coloring ★ – ★ ★ ★

Be it a fairy-like flower lamp or a shabby chic chandelier (see p. 61)—
these lamps brighten up any room in no time!

TOOLS AND MATERIALS

- Lightbulb holder without the shade
- Paper towel or toilet paper roll without the tissue
- A very short newspaper roll made from a 6-inch strip
- 4 normal newspaper rolls
- 10 newspaper rolls strengthened with wire (see p. 13)
- Glue stick
- For painting: acrylic paint, brush, container for the paint, an additional wire-strengthened paper roll, 4 sheets of printing paper

Tip

The toilet paper or paper towel roll serves as an aid for weaving—its diameter must be as big as the lightbulb holder.

FLOWER LAMP—HOW TO

1. Cover the pointed end of the very short newspaper roll with glue and insert it into the other end to make a ring that you place over the toilet paper roll or the lightbulb holder (fig. 1). It should easily fit over the toilet paper roll but not be too loose.

2. Push the ten wire-strengthened stakes between the ring and the toilet paper roll and bend the ends upward (fig. 2). Separate the stakes into pairs and space evenly around the toilet paper roll (fig. 3).

3. Use two newspaper rolls as the weavers and work them through the stakes and closely around the toilet paper roll. In doing so, always weave two stakes as one (fig. 4). When all four paper rolls have been woven, secure the ends of the weavers into the weave, using a pointed tool.

4. Press your fingers together and pull the stake ends through them to make the stakes more flexible. Insert the tips back into the opening from which the stake emerges. This is how you form the petals. Paint them pink with acrylic paint.

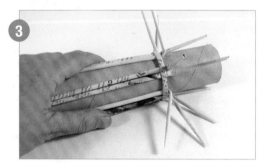

5. Use green (possibly slightly thinned) acrylic paint to paint the weave and the additional wire-strengthened paper rolls.

6. Crumple the four sheets of printing paper several times and then iron them smooth again. Thin some pink paint with water and paint the sheets pale pink. Once the paint on the paper has dried, you can use a thin brush to paint spots on the sheet, using unthinned pink paint (fig. 5). Do this on both the front and the back of the paper. Then allow to dry thoroughly.

7. Cover the paper rolls on the petal with glue and press a painted sheet of paper against it (use the paper sparingly). Once the glue has dried, use a pair of scissors to cut around the shape stakes (fig. 6). Repeat for all petals.

8. If you haven't done so already, now is the time to remove the toilet paper roll. Check whether there are any white spots that need painting, and attach the homemade shade to the lamp holder. Finally, insert the prepared green roll with the thick end into the weave and make a pretty vine around the lamp holder.

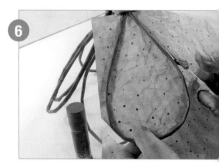

CHANDELIER—HOW TO

1. Carry out steps 1 to 3 as described for the flower lamp. However, use 12 wire-strengthened stakes (see p. 13) that you divide into six pairs.

2. Twist the stake pairs together for a few inches; approximately 8 inches from the weaving, wrap a piece of silver wire around the two stakes. Briefly curl the free ends tight around a pencil so that they form pretty flourishes and take on a chandelier shape.

3. Affix the lampshade to the holder and hang some glittery decorations in the "branches" in order to increase the glamour factor.

(see p. 13)

TOOLS AND MATERIALS

- The same material as for the flower lamp, but this time 12 wire-strengthened newspaper rolls
- Design: silver wire and scissors, a couple of plastic "crystals"

Woven Napkin Holders

Technical difficulty ★ ★   Time required ★   Coloring ★ – ★ ★

These napkin holders are a pretty accessory for any table. Make several variations so that they always match the rest of the table decoration.

TOOLS AND MATERIALS

- White and printed newspaper paper rolls (you will need 17 for three holders) (see p. 34)
- Paper towel roll without the tissue
- Rubber band
- Scissors
- Ruler or tape measure

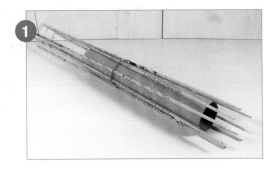

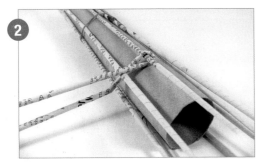

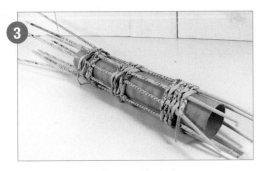

HOW TO

1. Position eight paper rolls around the kitchen roll and use a rubber band to secure them in place. Position the rolls so that they are approximately the same distance apart. The paper rolls form the spokes for the napkin rings (fig. 1).

2. Fold a paper roll in half and use it to start weaving the first napkin ring (see tip on p. 15 and fig. 2). Continue to weave until the ring's width is 10 inches. Push the weave closely together and cut off the remaining weavers.

3. At a little distance from the first napkin holder, start weaving the second and then the third napkin holder (fig. 3). Then remove the rubber band and pull out the paper towel roll.

4. Now position the three rings at equal distances on the spokes. There should be at least 2¾ inches of spoke on each side of the rings so that you can work a basket weave rim on each side. If a paper roll unravels after cutting, use a glue stick to glue it together.

5. Work the basket weave rim on each side, using the spokes (see p. 26 and fig. 4). Voilà! Following these steps should give you three napkin holders.

VARIATIONS

Pink Napkin Rings

Spray the finished napkin rings with Chalky Chic from Marabu (www.marabu-northamerica.com) in Powder Pink. With a matching ribbon, you can secure a name tag. I wrote the names on watercolor paper that I had painted small flowers on. Gluing the thin watercolor paper to a cardboard label, to which I added a metal eyelet for the ribbon, lends it an elegant and stable appearance.

Napkin Holder with Flowers

Take a thin strip of newspaper that is covered with printed text only, and fold it like a concertina. Cut one end into a point (fig. 5), unfold everything, and put glue on the long straight side. Pleat the strip in the shape of a flower and stick it to the bottom of the button (fig. 6). Sew or glue the button flower to the napkin ring.

Tip

Let your imagination run wild! Decorate the napkin holders with buttons and beads, embroider them with colorful ribbons, and embellish with glitter.

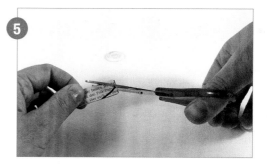

Candlelight in a Jar – Hanging Lamps

Technical difficulty ★ ★ Time required ★ Coloring ★

These pretty storm lamps are quick to make. They are great gifts, can add atmosphere to your garden party, or can lend a cozy feeling to your windowsill in winter—whatever you decide, they are a really special ornament.

TOOLS AND MATERIALS

- Newspaper rolls (approximately 15 per storm lamp)
- Jam jars (with an opening as big as possible) with straight sides
- Thick wire and pliers in order to bend a hook
- Optional: paint and wooden beads depending on storm lamp design

HOW TO

1. Lay out a cross of 4+4 spokes and weave a round basket base as described on p. 23.

2. Once the base is the size of the base of the jam jar, increase its size by a further round. Then fold the spokes vertically upward and weave two rounds.

3. Place the jam jar in the basket base and work one or two more rounds around the jar side (see tips on p. 19).

4. Cut the ends of the weavers and use a tool to tuck them into the weave.

5. Restart weaving farther up, by folding a paper roll in half and placing it around a stake (see tip on p. 15 and fig. 1).

6. Continue in this way until you reach the thread of the screw-top jar. Pay attention that you do not weave too tightly, so that you will be able to easily remove and clean the jar later.

7. Finally, weave a basket weave rim (see p. 26).

8. Use the pliers to bend the wire into a hanger and secure it in the weave.

VARIATIONS

White lamp with beads
For this lamp, you need completely white paper rolls (see p. 34). Make four spokes from very thin paper strips (7 cm wide), so that you can thread the wooden beads on them.

Make the spoke cross with four normal and four thin paper rolls. I framed each two thin rolls with two thick rolls. Continue according to the basic instructions until there is a break in the weaving.

Then thread a wooden bead onto each thin spoke. Begin the weaving farther up and carry onto the upper lip of the jar.

Newspaper lamp
For this lamp, make the rolls from normal newspaper. When rolling them, ensure that the print can be seen and there is not too much color (see p. 34).

At the place where the weaving is paused, position the spokes in the crossover pattern (fig. 2). Then fold the spoke back into the vertical position and weave the upper part.

Blue lamp
Work according to the basic instructions until the break in the weaving. For this design, insert a single row of weaving in the middle of the gap by starting to weave again with a roll bent in half. Secure the ends of the weavers where you started the round (fig. 3). Then weave the upper part as with the other two lamps. Finally, paint the finished storm lamp with Marabu Chalky Chic in Smokey Blue (fig. 4). If you want, you can also use some fine sandpaper to scuff the paint to give it a shabby chic look.

Tip
If you don't have any thick wire for the hanger but have only thin (silver) wire, you can use two lengths of it together. Twist the two lengths together and secure them in the weave of the storm lamp.

Spots and Stripes – Baskets with Lids

Technical difficulty ★ ★   Time required ★   Coloring ★ ★ – ★ ★ ★

These small baskets with lids can be made relatively quickly
with practice and are pretty storage jars for
all sorts of bits and bobs.

TOOLS AND MATERIALS

- Per basket, depending on size, 30 to 60 white newspaper rolls (see p. 34)
- Scissors
- Cylindric household item (tin, bottle, etc. as a form)
- Paint: Marabu Chalky Chic in Smoky Blue, Grey Blue, Light Blue, and White
- A thick-bristle brush and a fine hairbrush
- Masking tape

HOW TO

Basket

1. For small baskets whose diameter is to be less than 4 inches, make a spoke cross of 3+3 paper rolls. If you want to make a larger basket, then start with a spoke cross of 4+4 paper rolls (see p. 23).

2. Make a basket base that is slightly larger than the item that you are going to use as the form (see p. 18).

3. Place the item on the basket base and bend the spokes upward. Weave the basket side by weaving the weavers close to the form (see tip on p. 19).

4. At the desired height, finish with a simple tucked rim or a loop rim (see p. 26). These rims are not as thick as the basket weave rim, which in this case is important to ensure the lid fits well.

Lid

1. For the lid, make a basket base that is a little larger than the actual basket will be.

2. Turn the basket upside down and place it on the basket base. Fold the spokes of the base upward and weave a lip for the lid that is two or three rounds deep (fig. 1). Be careful that the lid lip does not end up too small, on account of the weave being slightly pulled together when finishing off. Only a flat rim is suitable to finish off the lid (i.e., the simple tucked rim [see p. 26] or the loop rim [see p. 26]). I used the tucked rim (fig. 2).

3. If you want, you can attach a small handle to the lid. To do so, pull a paper roll halfway through a hole in the top of the weave. Twist the two ends together before pushing them down through two holes that are close to each other in the weave of the lid. Cut the ends off on the inside of the lid and secure them in the weave of the lid or attach them with glue.

Color design

Paint the basket and lid in bright colors or use masking tape to make dots or stripes (see p. 34 and figs. 3–4). Use the fine brush to go over any rough edges. Look at each part from different angles to find any bits you missed.

Tip

If you like colorful stripes, then weave a striped basket using colored paper rolls. If you like, use the colors of the paper, or paint the paper rolls in advance to do so. You can see a pretty variation using a square basket base on p. 78.

Take a Seat – Seat Pad

Technical difficulty ★ ★ Time required ★ ★ Coloring ★ ★

It's surprising how much warmer it is when you sit on a pad of newspaper
instead of on naked wood or stone. Before you attempt this project,
you should have already made a few smaller objects with a woven base—
it takes a little practice to get the weave really tight.

TOOLS & MATERIALS

- Approximately 100 newspaper rolls per seat pad
- Wood varnish in white
- Wood varnish in rose pink
- Newspaper and scissors
- A thick-bristle brush and a fine brush

HOW TO

1. Make a spoke cross with 4+4 paper spokes. For this design, it is important that the paper spokes have exactly the same length. Secure the spoke cross by using the first paper roll, as described on p. 23. Check that all the spokes are protruding by the same amount; if they do not, then pull the short end out slightly. Now, continue to weave, at first weaving two spokes as one.

2. Separate the double spokes when the diameter of the circle is between 3 and 4 inches. Continue to weave in a circle.

3. After a couple of rounds (when the circle's diameter is approximately 6¼ to 8 inches), the distance between the spokes will be so large that it will be necessary to insert more spokes. In each space between spokes, work a paper roll that has been folded in half (see p. 18 and fig. 1); the two ends of the paper rolls will be worked as one in the first rounds of weaving after they have been inserted. Split them when the circle's diameter is approximately 11 inches.

4. When the shortest spoke is 1 to 1½ inches long, work a simple tuck rim (see p. 26). My seat pads have a diameter of 13 inches (fig. 2).

Color Design

The size of the seat pad lends itself to using a stencil template that you can download at www.pirlipause.de. Cut out the heart neatly. You will need both parts of the template: the paper heart and the paper with the hole for the cutout heart (see p. 37). You can paint the back of the pad either in a single color or also give it a design. If you make two seat pads, it looks particularly pretty when you make one heart white and the surrounding area pink, and for the other, the heart is pink and the surrounding area is white (fig. 3).

Information

The surface of the seat pad needs to meet a lot of requirements: the color should not rub off, it should tolerate at least a little water, and it should not suffer wear and tear too quickly. Therefore, I decided to use wood varnish as a protective coat. The wood varnish that I use is moisture resistant, and it takes 10 days to dry into a very resistant surface without becoming very stiff.

Tip

A woven mat has more uses than just a seat pad. It could serve as a table mat, be put under a plant, or be displayed as an ornament. Why not also try making one in an oval shape?

Small Square Basket

Technical difficulty ★ ★   Time required ★ ★   Coloring ★

Those of us who weave baskets from paper look forward to advertisement flyers in the mail (which normally annoy other people). Take a peek at what became of a glossy brochure with colored edges that recently landed in my mail.

TOOLS & MATERIALS

- Approximately 60 white paper rolls (see p. 34)
- 20–22 short white paper rolls (see p. 34)
- Colorful paper rolls in pretty colors from brochures, catalogs, or magazines (see p. 34)

HOW TO

1. Weave a square basket base with eight stakes as a basic frame (see p. 25). Weave around the stakes until you have a square base. My basket measures approximately 5½ × 5½ inches.

2. Pull the stakes so that they protrude equally on both sides.

3. On the two sides that do not have any stakes, insert six to seven short white stakes and start weaving the basket sides (fig. 1).

4. After a couple of rounds with white weavers, there should be a couple of colorful rounds. Change the color of both weavers in the same place where possible (i.e., extend the weavers with the colored rolls at the same place). So that this works, you could make some shorter rolls and insert them. After about five colorful rounds, change back to white weavers.

5. When your basket is approximately 2¾ inches tall, work in two handles according to the instructions on p. 32. For the upper part of both handles, use four short paper rolls as stakes on each side.

6. Weave three further rows before finishing off with a basket weave rim (see p. 26).

Newspaper Tote Bags

Technical difficulty ★★ Time required ★★–★★★ Coloring ★★

Tote bags are very useful to have around in day-to-day life.
If you make them yourself, you can determine the size and the color
to be just as you wish.

TOOLS & MATERIALS

For the Green Bag
- Approximately 90 newspaper rolls, at least 60 of which in white (see p. 34)
- A very thin newspaper roll in white (roll up 2¾-inch-wide strips) for the handle
- Marabu Chalky Chic spray paint in Mistletoe
- Clear varnish
- Jute cord
- Buttons

HOW TO

Green Bag

1. Weave an oval basket base from 3+4 spokes (*see right*) and work as described on p. 23. Use white spokes. The weavers may have print on them.

2. When the basket base has reached the desired size, fold the spokes vertically upward. Insert another spoke directly next to each spoke. Now weave the basket side, weaving the double spokes as one (fig. 1).

3. Once the basket sides have reached a height of 4¾ inches, paint them green with the spray paint. It will need two coats. Ensure that, where possible, the spokes remain white (fig. 2).

4. Now continue to weave with white rolls. Once your bag has reached the desired height, cut off the shorter paper roll from each pair of spokes (fig. 3). Use the remaining spokes to work a loop rim (see p. 26).

5. Insert the white knotted handles according to the instructions on p. 28.

6. Use the jute cord to sew a thin separating line between the green and white (fig. 4).

7. Decorate the bag with buttons or a tassel made of jute cord, according to your taste.

8. Finally, protect your bag against water and wear and tear by giving it a coat of varnish, paying particular attention to the handles. If the handles later become worn, you can simply remove them and attach new handles.

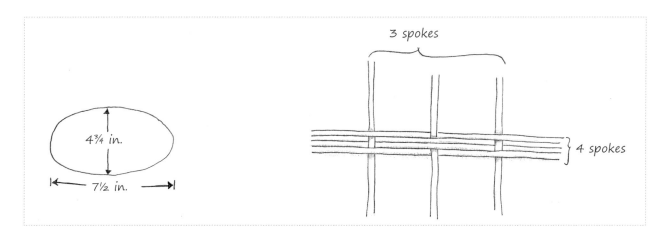

4¾ in.

7½ in.

3 spokes

4 spokes

HOW TO

Anchor Bag

1. Weave an oval basket base from 9+5 spokes, as described on p. 23 (see below).

2. Fold the spokes vertically upward and weave the basket side. In the corners, work an expanding shape. Don't weave the rounds directly over each other but bend the spokes a little outward and position the round of weaving slightly outside the previous one. When the distance between the spokes at the corners becomes too large, then work in four new spokes, two on each side (fig 1).

3. When the shortest spoke is still approximately 5 inches long, work a loop rim (see p. 26).

4. For the anchor motif, download the stencil template from my website (www.pirlipause.de) and position it in the center of the bag, in the manner described on p. 37. Protect the bag from water and wear and tear by giving it a coat of paint.

①

Inserted spokes

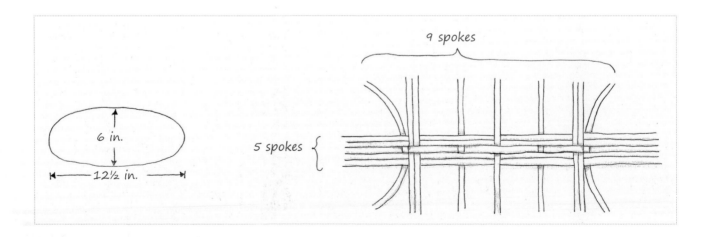

6 in.

12½ in.

5 spokes

9 spokes

Wastepaper Basket and Plant Pot

Technical difficulty ★ ★ ★　Time required　★ ★ ★　Coloring ★ ★ ★

Would you guess looking at these two baskets for the first time that (almost)
the only material used is newspaper? The combination of white and colored rolls
gives you so many design options.

TOOLS & MATERIALS

For the Wastepaper Basket
- Approximately 200–250 white rolls made of newspaper
- Approximately 25 colored rolls (see p. 34)
- A bucket or wastepaper basket to use as a form, and a weight to weigh it down
- Scissors
- Glue
- Optional: pegs
- Optional: protective varnish from Marabu

For the Plant Pot
- Approximately 25 prepainted blue rolls (see p. 34)
- Approximately 30 white rolls
- A container that you can weave around and that can later remain inside the basket (e.g., a large yogurt pot, an old plant pot, or a preserving can that is coated on the inside)

HOW TO

Wastepaper Basket

1. Weave a round basket base from a spoke cross of 4+4 spokes (see p. 23). If you are using a container as a form, work the spoke cross according to its dimensions. The basket base should have a somewhat larger diameter than the form.

2. Place the container on the basket base and bend the spokes upward. Remove the form and now weave the first rounds of the basket side. In doing so, place an additional spoke between every two spokes (fig. 1). Note that for the pattern on the basket, you need an uneven number of spokes, so if there is a big space between two spokes, add two spokes! Weave a couple of rounds so that the stakes are secure. Then place the weighed-down container in the basket and weave closely around it (see tip on p. 19).

3. Plan to start the crossover pattern at a height where the stakes do not need to be extended. It is now important that the two weavers are more or less the same length (if needed, make a short white roll and insert it). When the weavers run out, extend them with blue paper rolls (fig. 2) and weave one round. Then begin the crossover pattern by inserting two white parallel weavers between the blue crossover weavers (see p. 17). Work two rounds in the crossover pattern and finish off the white weavers. Weave another round with the blue weavers. Extend the weavers with white paper rolls again.

4. If the initial spokes get too short, extend the spokes according to the instructions on p. 13. If necessary, secure wobbly spokes to their neighbor by using a peg until the next round of weaving. Continue to work with white weavers until the extended spokes are fully woven in.

5. For the diagonal line pattern, simply weave a couple of rounds with one blue and one white weaver. Afterward, use two white weavers again.

6. For the blue stripes, extend the weavers at the same place with two blue paper rolls and weave one round with the two blue weavers.

7. Work a couple of rounds in all white and finally work a basket weave rim (see p. 26).

8. As a rule, a wastepaper basket doesn't have to withstand any great stresses and therefore does not necessarily need a protective coating. However, if you want, you can protect it with varnish.

Plant Pot

1. Work a round basket base from a spoke cross of 4+4 paper rolls (see p. 23) and weave around the cross with white paper rolls. When the base is slightly bigger than the form, fold the stake vertically up the form and weave two to three more rows, using white rolls.

2. Work a couple of rounds with the blue parallel weavers in the crossover pattern (see p. 17 and fig. 3).

3. To finish, weave a few more simple white rounds so that the crossover pattern has a pretty frame.

4. Complete the pot with a simple tucked rim (see p. 26).

Tip

For the plant pot, the size of the inner container determines whether you need to extend the spokes and how long the spoke ends are for the rim. If you have enough material for a basket weave rim, then you should choose this particularly decorative rim.

Source of Vitamins – A Fruit Bowl

Technical difficulty ★ ★ ★   Time required ★ ★ ★   Coloring ★ ★

For this project, you need space, time, and some prior experience
with basket weaving. Perhaps the most difficult thing
is creating a beautiful shape.

TOOLS & MATERIALS

- Approximately 150 white rolls made of newspaper, 8 short white rolls (see p. 34)
- Florist's wire
- PNZ wood varnish (safe for toys) and a soft brush
- Optional: a bowl as a form, heavy object to use as a weight

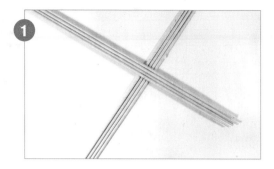

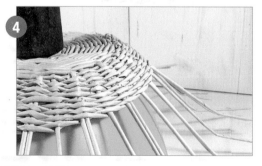

HOW TO

1. The diameter of the basket should be large, so you'll have to extend the spokes. Loosely insert a short white roll in each of the eight white paper rolls. Use these extended spokes to make a spoke cross (measure where the center is) and remove the short rolls for the time being (fig. 1). That makes the start of the weaving easier. Then finish the round basket base (p. 23). Follow the size of your form: mine had a diameter of 7¾ inches.

2. When the spokes of the initial spoke cross become too short, extend them again with the short rolls. When doing so, be sure to use a short piece of wire (see p. 13 and fig. 2)!

3. For weaving the basket sides, you have two options: You can bend the spokes upward and without using a form and weave a shape that expands outward. This option is recommended if you want your basket to have steeper sides. However, pay attention that the basket sides don't become too steep too soon.

Alternatively, you can place the basket base on top of an overturned bowl or a bucket and place a weight on top of it. Bend the stakes downward and weave the basket sides in a downward direction (figs. 3–4). In this way, it's easy to create a very open shape.

4. From a diameter of approximately 7¾ inches, insert a paper roll folded in half in every space between the spokes (see p. 18). Initially, weave the inserted pair of spokes as one. When the diameter of the basket expands further (e.g., after 2½ inches), divide the spoke pair and weave them individually.

5. To finish, work a basket weave rim (fig. 5). Thanks to the high number of spokes, it will have a beautiful thickness.

6. Finally, paint and protect the basket with a child-safe wood varnish of your choice (fig. 6). Be sure the varnish covers all the nooks and crannies.

Tip

Even if you want to give the fruit bowl a different appearance (weave in a pattern, leave newspaper print visible, etc.), you should still give it a coat of clear, child-safe wood varnish. This varnish means that it is suitable to be in contact with the fruit.

About the Author

I was born in 1977 and live with my husband, my three children, and a couple of hens and sheep in Ost Westfalen-Lippe, close to the Teutoberger Forest. Whether I am working on our house and garden, making music, writing creative texts, painting, crafting, drawing, or sewing, it's always a special joy to be creating something beautiful with my hands.

It makes me particularly happy to breathe new life into apparently worthless things and to give them a second chance.

You can visit me at my website at www.pirlipause.de. I look forward to hearing about and seeing your weaving projects.

Acknowledgments

Ms. Blum from the Wedegärtner bookshop in Steinheim: without you and your enthusiasm for my wonky and ugly baskets, my book would have likely never been written.

Sven Beckmann from Ringfoto Beckmann Schieder: many thanks for your photography workshop, which was tailored exactly to my needs.

Martina Unterfrauner, my project manager at Christophorus Verlag: You passionately supported my project from the very first moment. Thank you! It was very inspiring to work with you!

Anne Schulz, photographer: Thank you for the beautiful photos, which create exactly the right atmosphere.

Anne Köhler, reader: It was such a pleasure to polish my book project with you. (And how wonderful it would be if we could play the piano together one day!)

My husband, Joachim, and my three children: Your love and our life together are the foundations upon which my ideas grow and have been developed for this book. Jo, you deserve a special thank you for constantly giving me the freedom to work and for your practical support.

Sources

Chalky Chic chalk paint (spray paint and paint), Gessopinsel (a soft synthetic-bristle brush), water-based and solvent-based protective varnish: **Marabu Gmbh & Co. KG, www. marabu-northamerica.com**

Wood varnish in wood and bright colors (covering and glazing) and clear varnish: **PNZ, Die Holzpflege Manufakture, www. pnz.de, www.timberlove.blog**

Copyright © 2024 by Schiffer Publishing, Ltd.

Originally published as *Paper Baskets,* ©2021 Christophorus Verlag; Christian Verlag, Munich, Germany
Translated from the German by Catherine Venner

Library of Congress Control Number: 2023943017

Cover design by Ashley Millhouse
Photos: Anne Schulz
Step-by-step photos: Dorothea Katharina Schmidt
Type set in Black And White/Caecilia LT Pro

ISBN: 978-0-7643-6804-2
Printed in China

Published by Schiffer Publishing, Ltd.
4880 Lower Valley Road
Atglen, PA 19310
Phone: (610) 593-1777; Fax: (610) 593-2002
Email: Info@schifferbooks.com
Web: www.schifferbooks.com

For our complete selection of fine books on this and related subjects, please visit our website at www.schifferbooks.com. You may also write for a free catalog.

Schiffer Publishing's titles are available at special discounts for bulk purchases for sales promotions or premiums. Special editions, including personalized covers, corporate imprints, and excerpts, can be created in large quantities for special needs. For more information, contact the publisher.

We are always looking for people to write books on new and related subjects. If you have an idea for a book, please contact us at proposals@schifferbooks.com.